Tools

Search

Notes

Discuss
MyReportLinks.com Books
Go!

COLORADO

A MyReportLinks.com Book

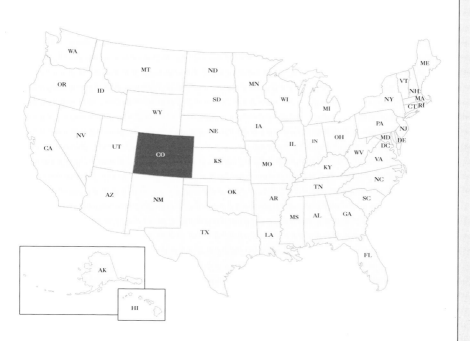

Stephen Feinstein

MyReportLinks.com Books

an imprint of

Enslow Publishers, Inc. E

Box 398, 40 Industrial Road
Berkeley Heights, NJ 07922
USA

MyReportLinks.com Books, an imprint of Enslow Publishers, Inc. MyReportLinks is
a trademark of Enslow Publishers, Inc.

Copyright © 2003 by Enslow Publishers, Inc.

All rights reserved.

No part of this book may be reproduced by any means
without the written permission of the publisher.

Library of Congress Cataloging-in-Publication Data

Feinstein, Stephen.
  Colorado / Stephen Feinstein.
    p. cm. — (States)
Summary: Discusses the land and climate, economy, government, and
history of the Centennial State. Includes Internet links to Web sites
related to Colorado.
Includes bibliographical references (p.) and index.
  ISBN 0-7660-5029-7
  1. Colorado—Juvenile literature. [1. Colorado.] I. Title. II.
Series: States (Series : Berkeley Heights, N.J.)
  F776.3.F45 2004
  978.8—dc21
                              2002014700

Printed in the United States of America

10 9 8 7 6 5 4 3 2 1

To Our Readers:
Through the purchase of this book, you and your library gain access to the Report Links that specifically back
up this book.
The Publisher will provide access to the Report Links that back up this book and will keep these Report Links
up to date on **www.myreportlinks.com** for three years from the book's first publication date.
We have done our best to make sure all Internet addresses in this book were active and appropriate when we
went to press. However, the author and the Publisher have no control over, and assume no liability for, the
material available on those Internet sites or on other Web sites they may link to.
The usage of the MyReportLinks.com Books Web site is subject to the terms and conditions stated on the
Usage Policy Statement on **www.myreportlinks.com**.
In the future, a password may be required to access the Report Links that back up this book. The password
is found on the bottom of page 4 of this book.
Any comments or suggestions can be sent by e-mail to comments@myreportlinks.com or to the address on
the back cover.

Photo Credits: America's Story from America's Library/Library of Congress, pp. 23, 42; Anasazi
Heritage Center, p. 13; Colorado State Archives, p. 29; Colorado.com/Jack Olson, pp. 22, 28; © Corel
Corporation, pp, 3 10; © 1995 PhotoDisc, pp. 11, 31, 35, 37, 41; DenverGov.Org, pp. 17, 45;
Enslow Publishers, Inc., p. 19; Explore-Rocky.com, pp. 20, 39; Library of Congress, p. 3
(Constitution); MyReportLinks.com Books, p. 4; National Park Service, p. 14; 14ers.com/©
1989–2002 Bill Middlebrook, pp. 25, 27.

Cover Photo: 1998 Corbis Corp.

Cover Description: Cliff Palace in Mesa Verde, Colorado.

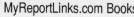
Contents

MyReportLinks.com Books
Great Books, Great Links, Great for Research!

MyReportLinks.com Books present the information you need to learn about your report subject. In addition, they show you where to go on the Internet for more information. The pre-evaluated Report Links that back up this book are kept up to date on **www.myreportlinks.com**. With the purchase of a MyReportLinks.com Books title, you and your library gain access to the Report Links that specifically back up that book. The Report Links save hours of research time and link to dozens—even hundreds—of Web sites, source documents, and photos related to your report topic.

Please see "To Our Readers" on the Copyright page for important information about this book, the MyReportLinks.com Books Web site, and the Report Links that back up this book.

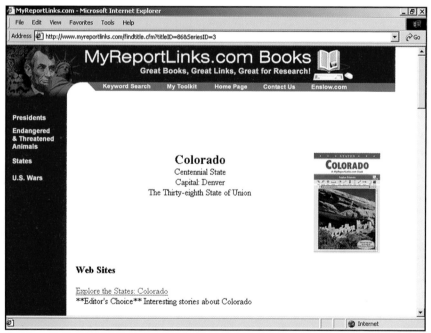

Access:

The Publisher will provide access to the Report Links that back up this book and will try to keep these Report Links up to date on our Web site for three years from the book's first publication date. Please enter **SCO7972** if asked for a password.

Report Links

 The Internet sites described below can be accessed at
http://www.myreportlinks.com

▶ **Explore the States: Colorado**   *EDITOR'S CHOICE
America's Story from America's Library, a Library of Congress
Web site tells the story of Colorado. Here you will learn about
some of Colorado's interesting traditions, such as the rodeo and
the Denver March Powwow.

Link to this Internet site from http://www.myreportlinks.com

▶ **Colorado Historical Society**   *EDITOR'S CHOICE
The Colorado Historical Society's Kid Page offers stories about the
people who influenced Colorado history. Here you will learn about
Barney Ford, Buffalo Bill, Kit Carson, and "Baby Doe" Tabor.

Link to this Internet site from http://www.myreportlinks.com

▶ **Mesa Verde National Park**   *EDITOR'S CHOICE
From the National Park Service Web site you will find a brief
description of Mesa Verde National Park located near Cortez and
Mancos, Colorado. Click on "inDepth" to view images of ancient
dwellings in Mesa Verde.

Link to this Internet site from http://www.myreportlinks.com

▶ **Canyons, Culture and Environmental Change**   *EDITOR'S CHOICE
Human occupation on the Colorado Plateau dates back twelve
thousand years. This Web site explores the people who lived on the
Colorado Plateau, the tools they used, and how the Plateau has
changed over the years.

Link to this Internet site from http://www.myreportlinks.com

▶ **Possibilities Colorado: Kids' Stuff**   *EDITOR'S CHOICE
At this Web site you will learn interesting facts about Colorado,
including why in 1976 Colorado refused to host the Winter Olympics.
You will also learn about "fourteeners" and general facts about the state.

Link to this Internet site from http://www.myreportlinks.com

▶ **Colorado**   *EDITOR'S CHOICE
Colorado is nicknamed the Centennial State, because it became the
thirty-eighth state to enter the Union on the United States one
hundredth birthday. This Web site explores Colorado's history prior to
its statehood.

Link to this Internet site from http://www.myreportlinks.com

Report Links

 The Internet sites described below can be accessed at
http://www.myreportlinks.com

▶ **Anasazi Heritage Center**
Discover the past at the Anasazi Heritage Center. Read about the Anasazi people, view photos of artifacts, and learn about archaeological sites. "Who Were The Anasazi?" tells how these ancient people lived.

Link to this Internet site from http://www.myreportlinks.com

▶ **Colorado Department of Natural Resources**
Avalanche! Learn about avalanches and how the state of Colorado issues warnings and predictions. While here, visit the Forestry section to view the department's Conservation Education section.

Link to this Internet site from http://www.myreportlinks.com

▶ **Colorado Division of Wildlife**
The Colorado Division of Wildlife presents information about hunting, fishing, habitat, and many other aspects of Colorado wildlife. Visit the "Kids' Page" where you will learn about Colorado's Mountain Lion and find fun games.

Link to this Internet site from http://www.myreportlinks.com

▶ **Colorado Fourteeners**
At this Web site you will find a comprehensive list of Colorado's fourteeners. You will also find images, descriptions, and learn about the animals that live on the mountains.

Link to this Internet site from http://www.myreportlinks.com

▶ **Colorado Historical Society**
Visit the Colorado Historical Society to learn about Colorado. By navigating through this site you can learn about architecture, archaeology, and find out what Centennial farms are.

Link to this Internet site from http://www.myreportlinks.com

▶ **Colorado Lore, Legend and Fact**
From the legend of "Baby Doe" to outlaws, you will find interesting information about lore and facts of Colorado. You can also view maps and photos of this beautiful state and its majestic mountains.

Link to this Internet site from http://www.myreportlinks.com

Report Links

 The Internet sites described below can be accessed at
http://www.myreportlinks.com

▶ **Colorado State Archives: Colorado Information and History**
The Colorado State Archives presents many interesting facts about the
"Centennial State." Here you can find out who Alfred Packer was and
why he became infamous. You can also read the 1867 state constitution
and view historical maps.

Link to this Internet site from http://www.myreportlinks.com

▶ **Colorado Trail**
This Web site provides information about Colorado's trails, including
facts, maps, events, and trail activities.

Link to this Internet site from http://www.myreportlinks.com

▶ **Colorado's Year of Trails**
At this Web site you can explore all aspects of Colorado's trails,
including historic trails such as the Cherokee Historic Trail and the
Continental Divide Trail.

Link to this Internet site from http://www.myreportlinks.com

▶ **DenverGov.Org**
View photos of Colorado's capital city. Included are images from
downtown Denver, parks, mountains, and more. Also included are
brief descriptions of the images.

Link to this Internet site from http://www.myreportlinks.com

▶ **Denver Museum of Nature and Science**
View photos of Colorado's new state mineral, read interviews with
space scientists, and get details about the Cedar Mountain Dinosaur
project. The museum also offers an archive of fascinating photos.

Link to this Internet site from http://www.myreportlinks.com

▶ **Discover Colorado**
The official Colorado state Web site offers a kid's section where you
will find information about Colorado's state emblems and symbols,
history, geography, government, and much more.

Link to this Internet site from http://www.myreportlinks.com

Report Links

The Internet sites described below can be accessed at
http://www.myreportlinks.com

▶ DoeHEADS Webpage
Read about the life of "Baby Doe," wife of Silver King Horace Tabor. This
rags-to-riches, to rags again, story has inspired songs, a movie, and an opera.
Photos and a list of related historical sites are included.

Link to this Internet site from http://www.myreportlinks.com

▶ Explore-Rocky.com
This Web site serves as a guide to Rocky Mountain National Park. Here you
can explore the park's trails, wildlife, and view panoramic images.

Link to this Internet site from http://www.myreportlinks.com

▶ Geology Field Notes: Dinosaur National Monument Colorado/Utah
The National Park Service Web site provides information about Dinosaur
National Monument in Colorado. Learn about the fossil bone deposits left
behind by the Stegosaurus and other dinosaurs.

Link to this Internet site from http://www.myreportlinks.com

▶ JohnDenver.com
Here you will find the biography of John Denver. Life in Colorado was the
inspiration for much of Denver's music.

Link to this Internet site from http://www.myreportlinks.com

▶ Nature: Grand Canyon
At this PBS Web site you will learn how the Colorado River helped form the
Grand Canyon, as well as other interesting facts about the Canyon's inhabitant
and history.

Link to this Internet site from http://www.myreportlinks.com

▶ NFL Internet Network: Denver Broncos
The official Denver Broncos Web site provides a complete history of the
Denver Broncos football team. Here you can view photos, statistics, and
interesting trivia about the Denver Broncos.

Link to this Internet site from http://www.myreportlinks.com

Report Links

 The Internet sites described below can be accessed at
http://www.myreportlinks.com

▶ Patricia Schroeder
Patricia Schroeder served in the United States House of Representatives
for twelve terms. At this Web site you will find a brief description of
her political career.

Link to this Internet site from http://www.myreportlinks.com

▶ PBS: Surviving the Dust Bowl
Experience the devastating Dust Bowl through eyewitness accounts and
photos. View a time line, maps, and learn about the catastrophe that
ravaged the Southern Plains.

Link to this Internet site from http://www.myreportlinks.com

▶ Reynolda House, Museum of American Art
German-born artist Albert Bierstadt brought the American West to life
with his beautiful landscapes. The beautiful scenery of Colorado
inspired many of his works. At this Web site you can read his
biography and view some of his most famous paintings.

Link to this Internet site from http://www.myreportlinks.com

▶ Stately Knowledge: Colorado
Here you will find basic facts about the state of Colorado, and
additional Internet resources.

Link to this Internet site from http://www.myreportlinks.com

▶ A Taste of Colorado History
Here you will find a collection of stories about Colorado and its
people. Some topics include stories about the gold rush, "Baby Doe,"
Tabor, Doc Holliday, and other interesting characters.

Link to this Internet site from http://www.myreportlinks.com

▶ U.S. Census Bureau: Colorado
At this Web site you will find the official census report on the state of
Colorado. Learn about the business, demographics, geography, and
population of this great state.

Link to this Internet site from http://www.myreportlinks.com

Colorado Facts

Capital
Denver

Population
4,301,261*

Gained Statehood
August 1, 1876, the thirty-eighth state.

Bird
Lark bunting

Tree
Colorado blue spruce

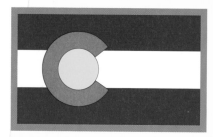

Flower
White and lavender columbine

Animal
Rocky Mountain bighorn sheep

Fish
Greenback cutthroat trout

Insect
Colorado hairstreak butterfly

Fossil
Stegosaurus

Song
"Where the Columbines Grow," words and music by Arthur J. Flynn.

Motto
"Nil sine Numine" (Nothing Without Providence)

Nickname
Centennial State

Flag
The state flag was adopted in 1911. The red C stands for Colorado, which is Spanish for "reddish" or "colored red." The golden ball inside the C represents Colorado's abundant sunshine and its production of gold. The blue and white bars symbolize Colorado's deep blue skies and snow-capped mountains.

*Population reflects the 2000 census.

Chapter 1

The State of Colorado

Colorado is located in the Rocky Mountain region of the western United States. The majestic Colorado Rockies are the state's claim to fame. Fifty-four of Colorado's mountain peaks are higher than 14,000 feet. The state's average altitude is the highest in the nation—about 6,800 feet above sea level. Denver, the capital, is known as "the Mile High

▲ Maroon Lake, located in a valley of the beautiful Maroon Bells, is so popular during the summer that the forest service is often forced to restrict vehicle traffic.

City." It sits at more than 5,000 feet above sea level, at the edge of the Rockies.

The mountains are a year-round attraction for Coloradans and the millions of visitors who come to the state each year. In winter, the snow is ideal for skiing, and the weather is generally dry and sunny. People also head for the mountains in the summer to cool off and enjoy the spectacular scenery.

The snow-capped Rocky Mountains may be the first thing that comes to mind when people think of Colorado. Yet not all of the state is mountainous. There are high, rolling plains in the eastern two fifths of the state. You can drive for many hours across these wide-open spaces without even seeing a mountain. The desert-like region west of the Rockies is made up of plateaus, mesas, and canyons.

▶ Coloradans Present and Past

The people of Colorado are as varied as the landscape. Most Coloradans, about 80 percent of the population, live in a narrow strip known as the Front Range Corridor. Just east of the Front Range of the Rockies, this corridor includes Colorado's largest cities—Fort Collins, Boulder, Denver, Colorado Springs, and Pueblo. About 75 percent of the people are Caucasian and 17 percent are Hispanic Americans. A small percentage are African Americans or Asian Americans.

Today, less than one percent of Colorado's population is American Indian. There was a time, though, when all the inhabitants of the area were American Indians. The remains of an ancient American Indian civilization can be seen at Mesa Verde National Park in southwestern Colorado, near the town of Cortez.

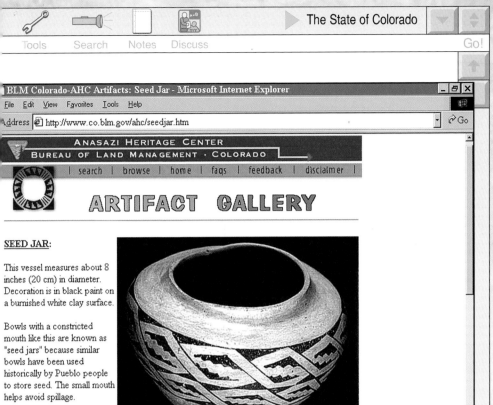

ANASAZI HERITAGE CENTER
BUREAU OF LAND MANAGEMENT · COLORADO

| search | browse | home | faqs | feedback | disclaimer |

ARTIFACT GALLERY

SEED JAR:

This vessel measures about 8 inches (20 cm) in diameter. Decoration is in black paint on a burnished white clay surface.

Bowls with a constricted mouth like this are known as "seed jars" because similar bowls have been used historically by Pueblo people to store seed. The small mouth helps avoid spillage.

Based on its design and material, this belongs to the

Internet

▲ *Anasazi, or Ancestral Puebloans as they are called today, produced and traded goods such as this seed jar.*

▶ Land of Dinosaurs

About 145 million years ago, dinosaurs roamed the earth. An especially popular place for dinosaurs was the northwestern corner of Colorado, which was then the eastern shoreline of a large, shallow sea. Dinosaurs liked to wade and graze in the swampy wetlands at the mouth of a river delta. The apatosaurus, diplodocus, and stegosaurus browsed among the ferns, palms, and other tropical vegetation. The flesh-eating allosaurus preyed upon these giant vegetarians.

Time and again, over millions of years, the river flooded. Thousands of dinosaurs were drowned and their carcasses became buried in a sand bar at the river's mouth. The sandy muck eventually hardened into sandstone, preserving the dinosaurs' bones as fossils.

More dinosaur fossils have been found in northwestern Colorado than anywhere else on earth. Hundreds of tons of dinosaur fossils have been excavated, and scientists are still finding dinosaur skeletons in the sandstone. Visitors can view fossils at Dinosaur Quarry in Dinosaur National Monument. The nearby town of Dinosaur has streets

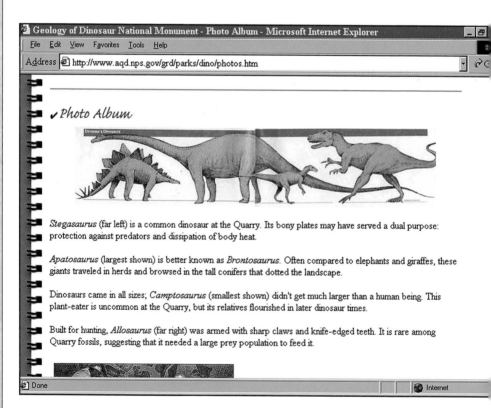

Geology of Dinosaur National Monument - Photo Album - Microsoft Internet Explorer

File Edit View Favorites Tools Help

Address http://www.aqd.nps.gov/grd/parks/dino/photos.htm

✔ *Photo Album*

Stegasaurus (far left) is a common dinosaur at the Quarry. Its bony plates may have served a dual purpose: protection against predators and dissipation of body heat.

Apatosaurus (largest shown) is better known as *Brontosaurus*. Often compared to elephants and giraffes, these giants traveled in herds and browsed in the tall conifers that dotted the landscape.

Dinosaurs came in all sizes; *Camptosaurus* (smallest shown) didn't get much larger than a human being. This plant-eater is uncommon at the Quarry, but its relatives flourished in later dinosaur times.

Built for hunting, *Allosaurus* (far right) was armed with sharp claws and knife-edged teeth. It is rare among Quarry fossils, suggesting that it needed a large prey population to feed it.

Done   Internet

Dinosaurs roamed the earth 145 million years ago. Now many, such as the stegosaurus, exist only as fossils at the Dinosaur National Monument in northwestern Colorado.

called Brontosaurus Boulevard, Plateosaurus Place, Stegosaurus Freeway, and Triceratops Terrace.

Inspired by the Mountains

Colorado's spectacular mountain scenery has inspired millions of people, including many writers, artists, and musicians. In 1893, Katherine Lee Bates (1859–1929) spent the summer as a visiting professor in Colorado. One day she took a ride on the cog railway to the top of Pikes Peak, where she was amazed by the view. To the east she could see the prairie stretching toward the distant horizon. In all other directions, the Rockies towered beneath an immense sky. She was inspired to write this poem:

> O beautiful for spacious skies,
> For amber waves of grain:
> For purple mountain majesties
> Above the fruited plain—
> America, America, God shed His grace on thee,
> And crown thy good with brotherhood
> From sea to shining sea . . .

Bates's poem "America the Beautiful" was soon set to music. Many Americans think of the song as a second national anthem.

Albert Bierstadt (1830–1902) is considered one of the greatest American romantic landscape painters. In 1859, he traveled around the Colorado Rockies for the first time. Awestruck by the mountains, he made sketches and took photographs while he traveled. Later he painted large panoramic views of the mountains based on his sketches and photos. Among his best-known paintings are "Morning in the Rocky Mountains," "Storm in the Rocky Mountains," and "Rocky Mountains—Landers Peak."

Henry John Deutschendorf, Jr., loved Denver and the Colorado Rockies so much that he changed his name to John Denver. In 1974, John Denver was named Colorado's poet laureate. His hits include, "Starwood in Aspen," "Rocky Mountain High," "Take Me Home Country Roads," and "Thank God I'm a Country Boy." Sadly, he died in a plane crash in 1997.

Chapter 2 ▶

Land and Climate

Colorado is the nation's eighth-largest state, with an area of 104,100 square miles. Wyoming and Nebraska lie to the north, Nebraska and Kansas to the east, New Mexico and Oklahoma to the south, and Utah to the west.

▶ Colorado's Four Regions

Colorado can be divided into four main geographic regions: the Rocky Mountains, the Colorado Plateau, the

▲ Home to Major League Baseball's Colorado Rockies since 1995, Coors Field holds more than 50,300 people.

Intermontane Basin, and the Great Plains. The Rocky Mountains run north to south through the middle of Colorado and occupy about two fifths of the state. The Colorado Rockies are part of a long mountain range that runs all the way from northwestern Canada to Mexico. In Colorado there are five main ranges of Rockies: the Front Range, Park Range, San Juan Mountains, Sangre de Cristo Mountains, and Sawatch Range.

The Front Range rises suddenly from the prairie, just west of Denver, Boulder, and Colorado Springs. This region includes some of Colorado's highest peaks—Mount Evans (14,264 feet), Longs Peak (14,255 feet), and Pikes Peak (14,110 feet). Rocky Mountain National Park is located in the Front Range. The Sangre de Cristo Mountains are just south of the Front Range. To the west of the Front Range is the Park Range, which contains Mount Elbert (14,433 feet), the highest mountain in Colorado. The Sawatch Range is south of the Park Range. The San Juan Mountains are in the southwestern part of the state.

There are four high, wide valleys in the mountains— level areas of open meadow known as "parks." They are called Middle Park, North Park, the San Luis Valley, and South Park. In 1843, a mountain man named Rufus Sage described one of the parks as an area of "beautiful lateral valleys, intersected by meandering watercourses, ridged by lofty ledges of precipitous rock, and hemmed in upon the west by vast piles of mountains climbing beyond the clouds. . . ."[1]

The poet Walt Whitman later described the view of South Park from the top of a mountain: "At this immense height the South Park stretches fifty miles before me. Mountainous chains and peaks in every variety of perspective, every hue of vista, fringe the view . . ."[2]

West of the Rockies is a desert-like region of plateaus, mesas, canyons, valleys, and hills. The northern part of the region is known as the Intermontane Basin. The word "intermontane" means "between mountains," and the area is indeed wedged between mountain ranges. Dinosaur National Monument is in this basin. The southern part of the region is known as the Colorado Plateau. Mesa Verde is located there, as is the national park called Black Canyon of the Gunnison, near the town of Montrose.

Colorado's Great Plains region lies east of the Rockies. The high, treeless plains are flat with some areas of low, rolling hills. The plains gradually rise in elevation from about 4,000 feet above sea level at Colorado's eastern border to anywhere from 5,000 to 6,000 feet where the

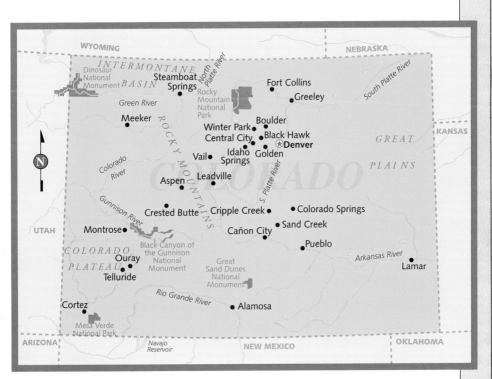

▲ A map of Colorado.

plains meet the Rockies. The lowest point in Colorado, 3,350 feet, is along the Arkansas River in Prowers County.

Much of the Great Plains region is now farmland. Yet it is possible to see what the prairie used to look like. Pawnee National Grassland, east of Fort Collins, and Comanche National Grassland, southeast of Pueblo, give a sense of the beauty of the plains before the settlers arrived.

▶ The Continental Divide

The Continental Divide winds down the spine of the Rockies through the middle of the state. It divides Colorado into two roughly equal parts—the Western

▲ This is a view of the Continental Divide taken at the Rocky Mountain National Park. The Continental Divide acts as a boundary between the Eastern and Western Slopes.

Slope and the Eastern Slope. All streams and rivers on the Western Slope flow west toward the Pacific Ocean. Water from the Eastern Slope flows toward the Gulf of Mexico or the Atlantic Ocean.

More than ten major rivers start in Colorado's Rockies. Among them are the Colorado, which flows westward, and the eastward-flowing Rio Grande, Arkansas, North Platte, and South Platte. Major John Wesley Powell explored the Colorado River and its tributaries from 1869 to 1872. In his book *The Exploration of the Colorado River and Its Canyons,* Powell describes the river's source in Grand Lake:

> A group of little alpine lakes, that receive their waters directly from perpetual snowbanks, discharge into a common reservoir known as Grand Lake, a beautiful sheet of water. Its quiet surface reflects towering cliffs and crags of granite on its eastern shore, and stately pines and firs stand on its western margin. The Green River . . . like the Grand, has its sources in alpine lakes fed by everlasting snows.[3]

▶ Plenty of Sunshine, Plenty of Snow

Many people think Colorado's climate is ideal. There are four distinct seasons. Colorful flowers bloom throughout the mountains in springtime. In the autumn, the aspen trees turn the mountainsides gold.

Summers are warm but pleasant, because the humidity is low. Every afternoon, like clockwork, there is a brief thunderstorm. The Rockies provide clear mountain air and cold streams and lakes for people who need to cool off. There is snow in the high mountains even in summer.

Winter brings snowstorms to the plains and heavier snow to the mountains, as much as four hundred inches a year. Skiers come from far and wide, drawn by the deep

Back   Forward   Stop   Review   Home   Explore   Favorites   History

COLORADO.COM

PHOTO BY JACK OLSON

Done   Internet

▲ *The brilliant colors of autumn bring the mountainside aglow.*

powder snows. Occasional cold spells bring extremely low temperatures, but the winter weather is usually not unpleasant. The air is dry, and there is lots of sunshine. Colorado has more than three hundred days of sunshine a year. At high altitudes, the winter sun warms the thin air quickly.

Precipitation averages fifteen inches a year. The average temperature is 28°F in January and 74°F in July. The record low temperature of −61°F occurred at Maybell in Moffat County on February 1, 1985. The record high temperature of 118°F was at Bennett on July 11, 1888.

Chapter 3

Economy

There has been a series of boom-and-bust cycles in Colorado as industries have grown and declined. Each boom brought hordes of people to the state, hoping to make their fortunes. There was a gold boom in the 1860s, a silver boom in the 1870s, and another gold boom in the 1890s. Meanwhile, coal mining grew, followed by an oil

▲ Many people came to Colorado hoping to become rich by mining for gold in the 1860s and 1890s.

boom in the 1920s and a uranium boom in the 1950s. There was a second oil boom during the energy crisis of the 1970s and early 1980s.

Colorado's Thriving Economy

Happily, Colorado's economy no longer depends on a single industry. Service industries employ more than 80 percent of the state's workers. Colorado's service industries include finance, insurance, real estate, computer software, engineering, law, and retail shops. Especially important are businesses that cater to tourists, such as hotels, ski resorts, and restaurants.

About 7 percent of Coloradans work in construction jobs and about 8 percent in manufacturing jobs. The most important areas of manufacturing are computer and electronic products, medical instruments, and food processing. The nation's third-largest beer brewer, the Coors Brewing Company, is located in Golden, Colorado.

At one time, nearly every worker in Colorado was employed in the mining industry. In 2002, only about one percent of the state's workers had jobs in mining. However, Colorado is still an important provider of resources, including coal, natural gas, and oil. The huge Hugoton gas field, located in the eastern plains, is one of the nation's richest sources of natural gas. Colorado's mines still produce gold and silver, as well as copper, lead, molybdenum, and zinc. The nation's only operating diamond mine is located along the Colorado–Wyoming border.

Only about 3 percent of Coloradans work on farms, but the state is an important producer of beef cattle and sheep. Field crops include beans, corn, hay, potatoes, sugar beets and wheat. Apples, grapes, and peaches are grown on the Colorado Plateau.

▶ "For Purple Mountain Majesties"

More than 25 million people visit Colorado each year for business or pleasure. They are mainly drawn by the Rocky Mountains. President Theodore Roosevelt, commenting on Colorado's amazing views, said, "The scenery bankrupts the English language."[1] Many other visitors find themselves speechless when they see the Rockies for the first time.

One of the best places to see the high peaks is Rocky Mountain National Park. Located just northwest of Boulder, the park has towering mountains and crystal-clear lakes. Elk graze in valleys surrounded by forests of ponderosa pine. Visitors can drive across the Continental Divide on

http://www.14ers.com/photos/MorePhotos/SandDunes/200010_GreatDunes_05a.jpg - Microsoft Internet ...

File   Edit   View   Favorites   Tools   Help

Address http://www.14ers.com/photos/MorePhotos/SandDunes/200010_GreatDunes_05a.jpg   Go

Done   Internet

▲ Colorado's sand dunes have reached as high as nine hundred feet.

Trail Ridge Road. This road climbs above twelve thousand feet and is one of the highest roads in the nation. Above the timberline, the road winds across an alpine tundra that resembles the Arctic region of Alaska. There are also roads to the top of Pikes Peak and Mount Evans.

Many other amazing sights await visitors to the Rockies. Royal Gorge, near Cañon City in the Sangre de Cristo Range, is one of the deepest canyons. A suspension bridge, the highest in the world, crosses the gorge 1,053 feet above the Arkansas River. Tourists can drive across the bridge, walk across it, ride across the gorge on an aerial tramway, or ride an incline railway down to the river. Further south in the Sangre de Cristos, near the town of Alamosa, is Great Sand Dunes National Monument. These dunes rise as high as nine hundred feet, the highest in the nation. The 50-square-mile expanse of sand seems out of place in the Rockies. It is almost as if a section of the Sahara Desert had been transported to Colorado.

Just west of Colorado Springs is the strange and beautiful Garden of the Gods. In the 1880s, novelist Helen Hunt Jackson described its giant red sandstone rock formations as "colossal monstrosities looking like elephants, like gargoyles, like giants . . . all motionless and silent . . ."[2] Although the rocks may look monstrous, they are popular with climbers.

Along with mountain climbing and hiking, Colorado's Rockies offer a variety of activities. Especially popular are whitewater rafting, sailing on mountain lakes, mountain biking, fishing, and horseback riding at dude ranches. Many tourists enjoy narrow-gauge train rides along steep cliff sides and through deep canyons. Others take four-wheel-drive tours of remote mountain passes and ghost towns. Many mining towns, abandoned when boom times

http://www.14ers.com/photos/MorePhotos/GardenGods/200001_Garden_01a.jpg - Microsoft Internet Expl...

File Edit View Favorites Tools Help

Address http://www.14ers.com/photos/MorePhotos/GardenGods/200001_Garden_01a.jpg   Go

Done   Internet

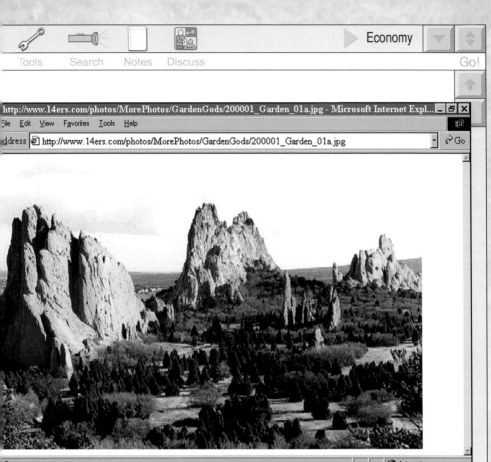

▲ Rock formations consisting of red sandstone make up the Garden of the Gods.

ended, became ghost towns. Some historic mining towns, such as Central City and Leadville, have been restored. Others, such as Aspen and Telluride, have become major ski resorts.

Skiing is at the top of Colorado's long list of outdoor activities. World-class ski resorts include Aspen, Crested Butte, Steamboat Springs, Telluride, Vail, and Winter Park. Skiers are attracted by the beauty of the mountains and the special qualities of Colorado's snow, which is drier, lighter, and softer than snow in the mountains of New England or California.

Hunting and fishing are also popular. More than 15 million rainbow, brown, brook, and cutthroat trout are caught each year in Colorado's mountain streams. Hunters go after bighorn sheep, black bears, elk, mountain goats, pronghorn antelope, white-tailed and mule deer.

◄ *Coloradans can expect up to four hundred inches of snow in the winter. This is one reason why skiers are particularly drawn to this area of the country.*

Government

On August 1, 1876, Colorado became the thirty-eighth state to be admitted to the Union. That year, the United States was celebrating its centennial, the nation's one-hundredth birthday. In honor of this event, Colorado was nicknamed the Centennial State.

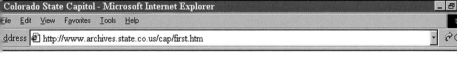

Colorado State Capitol - Microsoft Internet Explorer

File   Edit   View   Favorites   Tools   Help

ddress http://www.archives.state.co.us/cap/first.htm   ⏷ Go

The Colorado State Capitol Building Site

By Jason Brockman, Staff Archivist
Erin McDanal, Webmaster/Editor

🌐 Internet

▲ *The Colorado State Capitol Building holds the governor's office as well as the chambers for the state senate and house of representatives.*

▶ Colorado's Constitution

Colorado's constitution was adopted the same year. It outlines the structure of the state government and the powers of the various branches and departments. Colorado is still governed by its first constitution, but the document has been amended, or changed, about one hundred times.

▶ The Structure of Colorado's Government

The state government is divided into three branches—legislative, executive, and judicial. The legislative branch creates the laws, the executive branch carries out the laws, and the judicial branch interprets the laws.

The chief executive is the governor, who is elected by the voters to a four-year term of office. The governor may serve a maximum of two consecutive terms. The lieutenant governor is also elected to a four-year term, with a limit of two consecutive terms. Colorado's voters each cast one vote for both officials.

Three other officials of the executive branch—the secretary of state, the attorney general, and the treasurer—are elected to four-year terms. Like the governor and lieutenant governor, they can serve a maximum of eight consecutive years in office. The governor appoints the directors of other departments. The state senate must approve of these appointments.

The legislative branch of Colorado's state government consists of a senate with thirty-five members and a house of representatives with sixty-five members. Senators are elected to four-year terms. Representatives are elected to two-year terms. Both senators and representatives are limited to eight consecutive years in office.

The judicial branch of Colorado's government consists of the state supreme court, the court of appeals, twenty-two district courts, county courts, and municipal courts in the larger towns. The state supreme court consists of a chief justice and six associate justices who are appointed by

▲ *Truly modern, Denver was the first major city to allow women the right to vote.*

the governor. After beng appointed, a justice serves two years. A justice may serve additional ten-year terms, but must be approved by the voters each time.

▶ Colorado Women and Minorities in Politics

In 1893, Denver became the world's first major city to allow women to vote. In more recent times, Coloradans elected Patricia Schroeder to represent them in the U.S. House of Representatives. She served there for twenty-four years. As of 2002, no other woman had served in the House as long.

Federico Peña, a Mexican American, was elected to two consecutive terms as mayor of Denver, from 1983 to 1991. In 1993, President Bill Clinton appointed Peña to head the U.S. Department of Transportation. In 1997, she became head of the U.S. Department of Energy.

In 1992, Ben Nighthorse Campbell was elected to represent Colorado in the U.S. Senate. Campbell became the first American Indian U.S. senator.

History

Sometime more than twenty thousand years ago, nomadic hunters from Asia began migrating from Siberia to Alaska. Sea levels were much lower during the last Ice Age, and a land bridge extended across what is now the Bering Sea. The hunters followed herds of wild animals across the land bridge. By about 10,000 B.C., the Ice Age was ending, and the thick sheets of ice covering much of North America were retreating. The nomadic hunters, called Paleo-Indians by archaeologists, wandered south. Groups of Paleo-Indians reached what is now Colorado after 10,000 B.C.

▶ Ancient Coloradans

The Paleo-Indians in Colorado hunted animals, including giant ground sloths, woolly mammoths, and mastodons. Paleo-Indian spearheads, known as Folsom points, have been found on the western slope of the Rockies near Montrose and throughout Colorado's southeastern plains.

As the climate warmed, the Paleo-Indians adjusted to the changing conditions. They became hunter-gatherers, hunting smaller game and gathering berries, fruits, and nuts. The first settlements in Colorado were built by descendants of the Paleo-Indians known as the Anasazi. The Anasazi developed a farming culture and grew corn, beans, and squash in irrigated fields. They made tightly woven baskets of dried grasses and are sometimes called the "Basket Makers."

The Anasazi, also called the Ancestral Puebloans, began living at Mesa Verde around A.D. 550. Mesa Verde ("Green Table" in Spanish) is a plateau that rises 1,600 feet above the surrounding countryside. Canyons slice through parts of the top of the plateau.

Between A.D. 750 and 1100, the Anasazi built apartment houses out of rock or mud bricks on the mesa top. After A.D. 1100, they started building cliff dwellings. Many of the eight hundred cliff dwellings at Mesa Verde are several stories high. One building, known as Cliff Palace, contains two hundred rooms and twenty-three kivas. A *kiva* is a round ceremonial meeting place.

Around A.D. 1300, the Anasazi mysteriously disappeared. Nobody knows why they abandoned the cliff dwellings, but a severe drought that lasted many years is a likely reason. The Anasazi probably wandered south into what is now New Mexico and joined other groups of people. They may well be the ancestors of today's Pueblo peoples—the Acoma, Sandia, Taos, and Zuni.

While the Anasazi were building their civilization at Mesa Verde, other groups of native peoples lived elsewhere in Colorado. The Ute lived in the valleys of the Rocky Mountains. East of the Rockies were the Plains Indians, including the Arapahoe, Cheyenne, Comanche, and Kiowa. Other Colorado tribes included the Navajo, Pawnee, and Sioux. In time, all of these peoples would face changes in their way of life with the arrival of the European settlers.

Explorers, Traders, and Trappers

The first Europeans to arrive in what is now Colorado were probably from Spain. In 1541, Francisco Vásquez de Coronado was searching for the Seven Cities of Cibola,

▲ *The Ancestral Puebloans lived year-round in cliff dwellings located in what is now Mesa Verde National Park.*

fabled for their legendary wealth. Members of his expedition wandered north from New Mexico into Colorado.

In the 1600s, the Spanish took control of New Mexico and established Santa Fe and other settlements. They traded with the natives of Colorado, exchanging iron pots, rifles, steel needles, and whiskey, for furs and hides.

By around 1700, the Ute had acquired horses from the Spanish. The horse became an important part of the Ute lifestyle. With horses they could travel faster and cover greater distances. Within another fifty years, all the Colorado American Indian tribes would have horses.

The Spanish and French had a long tug of war over Colorado. In 1682, a French explorer named René-Robert

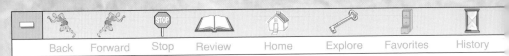
Cavelier, Sieur de la Salle, claimed a large area of North America for France. The area, which included the eastern part of Colorado, was called Louisiana. In 1706, Juan de Ulibarri claimed Colorado for Spain. In 1762, France gave to Spain all of its land west of the Mississippi River. Spain, then, agreed to give the land back to France in 1801. In 1803, President Thomas Jefferson bought the Louisiana Territory from France for $15 million. The Louisiana Purchase, which included eastern and central Colorado, doubled the size of the United States.

During the next twenty years, American explorers led expeditions throughout the Louisiana Territory. In 1806, Zebulon M. Pike, an officer in the U.S. Army, led an expedition through the Rocky Mountains. When he first saw Pikes Peak, he declared that nobody would ever be able to climb it.

In 1820, Major Stephen H. Long led an expedition across the Great Plains and through the Rockies. While crossing the plains, Long compared the area to the great sandy deserts of North Africa. He called the plains the "Great American Desert" and said crops would never be grown there. Later, of course, settlers turned the plains into the "Breadbasket of the World." Long traveled as far west as Royal Gorge. Longs Peak in Rocky Mountain National Park is named after him.

In 1821, Mexico won its independence from Spain, and western Colorado became a part of Mexico. Trade between the United States and Mexico quickly developed. The Santa Fe Trail—from St. Louis, Missouri, to Santa Fe, New Mexico—passed through the southeastern part of Colorado. The trail served as a major trade route.

Trading posts and forts were established along the trail. Traders, trappers, mountain men, Mexicans, Americans,

French, and Indians would gather at such places. Kit Carson, the famous frontiersman, traded beaver pelts at Bent's Fort near Las Animas, Colorado.

In 1846, bitter border disputes between the United States and Mexico led to war. In 1848, a defeated Mexico signed the Treaty of Guadalupe-Hidalgo. This treaty gave its vast northern territories, including western Colorado, to the United States. All of Colorado now belonged to the United States.

▶ "Pikes Peak or Bust"

Few Americans settled in Colorado until late in the 1850s. Then, in 1858, gold was discovered west of what is now Denver, at Dry Creek. Colorado's first boom had begun. At least fifty thousand gold seekers streamed into the state.

▲ Founded in 1860, Denver has become a sprawling metropolis on the edge of the Rocky Mountains.

The slogan "Pikes Peak or Bust" was painted on many covered wagons that traveled west across the plains. A few prospectors became rich panning for gold in the mountain streams, but most were lucky not to starve to death. Some people made a fortune by providing food and other supplies to the prospectors and miners. Mining towns such as Black Hawk, Central City, and Idaho Springs sprang up in the mountains. Denver was founded in 1860 and quickly became the commercial center of the Front Range.

In 1859, Coloradans established their own government. They asked the U.S. Congress to recognize Colorado as the Jefferson Territory. Congress refused, and in 1861 named the area the Colorado Territory.

During the 1860s and 1870s, farmers and ranchers settled on Colorado's eastern plains and in fertile river valleys west of the Rockies. The federal government signed treaties with the American Indians, promising that they could live in peace on reservations. Unfortunately, the treaties were often broken. American miners, farmers, and ranchers believed they had more right to Colorado's lands than the American Indians. Conflict soon developed.

The Arapaho and Cheyenne Indians depended on the buffalo for food and other needs. New settlers on the plains hunted buffalo for sport, killing enormous numbers of them. Fighting broke out as groups of American Indian warriors attacked wagon trains. The U.S. Army, in turn, attacked the Indians. In 1864, the Cheyenne Chief Black Kettle appealed for peace. The army promised to protect the Cheyenne if they would camp at Sand Creek. The Cheyenne did so, but were attacked there by a 700-man army led by Colonel John Chivington. The Cheyenne village was destroyed, and about five hundred Cheyenne were killed, most of them women and children. This shameful episode became known as the Sand Creek Massacre.

In spite of these problems, settlers continued to stream into the territory. In 1870, Horace Greeley, owner of the *New York Tribune,* published his famous advice "Go West, young man."[1] Greeley was interested in developing the West and financed a farming colony in Colorado that later became the town of Greeley.

Thousands of other people followed Greeley's advice. The arrival of the railroad made the West more accessible. In 1870, the Denver Pacific Railroad and the Kansas Pacific Railroad linked Colorado with the East. Cowboys

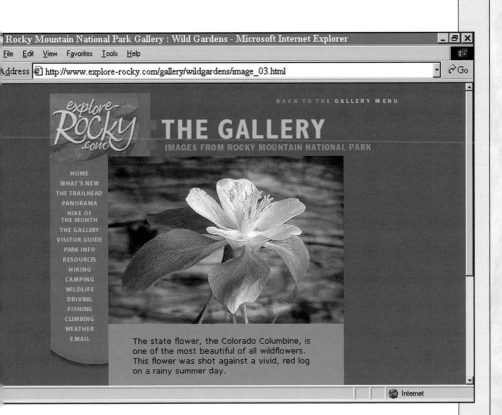

The Columbine is Colorado's state flower.

drove great herds of cattle across the plains from Texas to railheads in Colorado and Kansas.

More settlers meant more conflict with the Indians. When the gold-mining boom ended, the government hoped to persuade people to stay in Colorado. The government forced the American Indians to sell much of their reservation lands. Settlers were each given 160 acres of the land taken from the American Indians free of charge. The settlers were required only to farm the land or plant trees on it.

In 1878, Nathan Meeker, who had managed Horace Greeley's farming colony, took a new job. He became reservation agent for the White River Ute Indian Agency in northwestern Colorado. Meeker aimed to persuade the Ute Indians to give up their traditional lifestyle and to live as Christian farmers. By the following year, it was clear to Meeker that the Ute would not follow his suggestions. So Meeker called in troops. The Ute, fearing the troops planned to massacre them, killed Meeker and ten employees. The incident, known as the Meeker Massacre, outraged the settlers. The Ute Chief Ouray argued for peace between the two sides without success. The Ute were banished to new reservation lands in the deserts of Utah and a small reservation in southwestern Colorado. The Ute called their trek into the desert the "Trip of Sorrow."

Silver Boom and Bust

On August 1, 1876, Colorado was admitted to the Union. At the time, the state was in the midst of a silver boom. Silver had been discovered near Leadville several years earlier and Aspen, Cripple Creek, Leadville, and other mining towns were now booming.

▲ *A passenger train rolls through the Colorado countryside.*

Horace A. Tabor became known as the Silver King. He used the wealth from his Matchless Mine near Leadville to build elegant opera houses and other buildings in Leadville. He also helped to build Denver into a major financial center. Tabor became a U.S. senator and married the beautiful Elizabeth "Baby Doe" McCourt. President Chester A. Arthur attended their wedding.

For several years, Tabor and Baby Doe enjoyed a lavish lifestyle. In 1893, however, a financial panic caused silver prices to collapse. The Colorado silver boom became a bust. Many busy mining towns became ghost towns practically overnight.

As for Tabor, his mine was now worthless, and he and Baby Doe were broke. Tabor died penniless in 1899. The Matchless was foreclosed by the bank. For the rest of her life, Baby Doe lived in poverty in a wooden shack near the

▲ Elizabeth "Baby Doe" Tabor was considered to be one of the most beautiful women of her time.

entrance to the mine. One bitter cold winter day in 1935, she froze to death.

Composer Douglas Moore turned the story of the Tabors into an opera, "The Ballad of Baby Doe," which premiered in 1956. Visitors to Leadville today can visit the Tabor Opera House and the Tabor Grand Hotel.

▶ A Century of Growth

Colorado continued to grow throughout the twentieth century. By 1910, Colorado had more irrigated land than any other state, and agriculture replaced mining as the state's most important industry. The major crops were potatoes, sugar beets, and wheat. During World War I, prices for farm products were high. So farmers borrowed money to buy more farmland.

While farmers grew their crops, other Coloradans turned to a new resource—oil. Demand for oil continued to grow with the popularity of the automobile. By 1920, oil had become the most important mineral in the state. Drilling expanded with the oil boom of the 1920s.

Like most of America, Colorado was devastated by the Great Depression during the 1930s. Many people lost their jobs. Farmers were hurt when prices for agricultural products fell. A long and severe drought caused havoc on the plains. Crops failed and strong winds blew away the topsoil, whipping it into blinding dust storms. Large areas of the Great Plains in Colorado and neighboring states became known as the "Dust Bowl."

Colorado's economy revived during World War II. Manufacturing boomed, especially for war-related products, and several military bases were established in the state. There was a uranium-mining boom in western Colorado. After the war, the state's population grew very rapidly. Suburbs sprang up around the larger cities.

By 1954, manufacturing had replaced agriculture as the state's leading industry. Defense-related products were especially important. The U.S. Air Force Academy opened at Colorado Springs in 1958. In 1966, the North American Aerospace Defense Command was completed near Colorado Springs. It is located 1,200 feet underground in Cheyenne Mountain.

In the 1970s, the United States experienced a major energy crisis. Drilling activities in Colorado were stepped up, and the oil boom started, bringing more new workers. The Union Oil Company of California started major oil

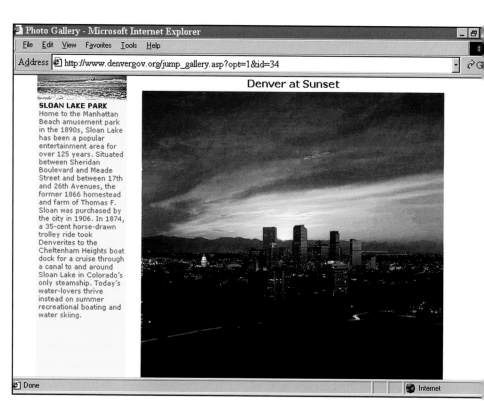

Photo Gallery - Microsoft Internet Explorer

File Edit View Favorites Tools Help

Address ⮡ http://www.denvergov.org/jump_gallery.asp?opt=1&id=34

Denver at Sunset

SLOAN LAKE PARK
Home to the Manhattan Beach amusement park in the 1890s, Sloan Lake has been a popular entertainment area for over 125 years. Situated between Sheridan Boulevard and Meade Street and between 17th and 26th Avenues, the former 1866 homestead and farm of Thomas F. Sloan was purchased by the city in 1906. In 1874, a 35-cent horse-drawn trolley ride took Denverites to the Cheltenham Heights boat dock for a cruise through a canal to and around Sloan Lake in Colorado's only steamship. Today's water-lovers thrive instead on summer recreational boating and water skiing.

Done   Internet

▲ *Denver, Colorado's state capital, sits at the base of the Rocky Mountains.*

shale operations near the town of Parachute in western Colorado. The company believed that the high oil prices would make it worthwhile to extract oil from shale. By 1982, the economy had slowed, and the price of oil had dropped. The oil shale dreams evaporated, and the project closed down. The oil boom in Colorado was over.

By the mid-1990s, Colorado had become one of the fastest-growing states in the country. Tourism was a major factor. Also, many new high-tech businesses were established in Denver and other cities. New high-rise towers rose above Denver.

Growth has brought problems as well as opportunity. Denver was once known for its clean, healthy air. The enormous growth in population meant more traffic and pollution. On some days, Denver now sits beneath a brownish haze of smog. In 1986, the Environmental Protection Agency (EPA) said that Denver led the nation in carbon-monoxide pollution. On days when pollution levels are high (usually in winter), Denver residents are not allowed to burn wood in their fireplaces. They are asked to use public transportation to decrease exhaust fumes from cars.

Columbine Massacre

A horrific and unexpected problem occurred on April 20, 1999. Columbine High School in Littleton, Colorado, was the scene of the deadliest school shooting in American history. Two students that considered themselves to be outcasts, opened fire on their classmates leaving thirteen people dead and twenty-five injured. People across the United States were stunned by the tragic incident.

Tourism and the Environment

The growth in tourism also brings problems. Rocky Mountain National Park has been overwhelmed by huge numbers of visitors and must build new roads and facilities. Hikers and backpackers in wilderness areas are asked to stay on the main trails, because taking shortcuts causes severe erosion.

Coloradans must work to protect the quality of their air, water, and natural surroundings. This will ensure that Colorado continues to be the exciting and beautiful land of "purple mountain majesties."

Chapter 2. Land and Climate

1. Rufus Sage, as quoted in Michael T. Smithson, *Rocky Mountain: The Story Behind the Scenery* (Las Vegas: KC Publications, 1986), p. 42.

2. Walt Whitman, as quoted in Sarah Lovett, *Unique Colorado* (Santa Fe: John Muir Publications, 1993), p. 63.

3. J. W. Powell, *The Exploration of the Colorado River and Its Canyons* (New York: Dover Publications, Inc., 1961), p. 17. (Originally published by Flood & Vincent in 1895 under the title *Canyons of the Colorado.*)

Chapter 3. Economy

1. Theodore Roosevelt, as quoted in Bruce Caughey and Dean Winstanley, *The Colorado Guide: Landscapes, Cityscapes, Escapes* (Golden, Colo.: Fulcrum, Inc., 1989), p. 1.

2. Helen Hunt Jackson, as quoted in Stephen Metzger, *Colorado Handbook* (Chico, Calif.: Moon Publications, Inc., 1999), p. 198.

Chapter 5. History

1. Greeley Convention and Visitors Bureau, "Greeley History," *About Greeley, 1997–2002*, <http://www.greeleycvb.com/history.shtml> (October 22, 2002).

Aylesworth, Thomas G., and Virginia L. Aylesworth. *The Southwest: Colorado, New Mexico, Texas.* Broomall, Pa.: Chelsea House Publishers, 1995.

Blashfield, Jean F. *Colorado.* 2nd ed. Danbury, Conn.: Children's Press, 1999.

Bledsoe, Sara. *Colorado.* Minneapolis: Lerner Publishing Group, 2002.

Epstein, Vivian S. *History of Colorado's Women for Young People.* Denver, Colo.: V S E Publisher, LLC, 1997.

Harris, Richard. Hidden *Colorado.* Berkeley, Calif.: Ulysses Press, 1996.

Jackson, Helen Hunt, and Mark I. West, ed. *Bits of Colorado: Helen Hunt Jackson's Writings for Young Readers.* Palmer Lake, Colo.: Filter Press, LLC, 2000.

Klusmire, Jon. *Colorado.* Oakland, Calif.: Compass American Guides, Inc., 1993.

Lovett, Sarah. *Unique Colorado.* Santa Fe: John Muir Publications, 1993.

Metzger, Stephen. *Colorado Handbook.* Chico, Calif.: Moon Publications, Inc., 1999.

Miller, Amy. *Colorado.* Danbury, Conn.: Children's Press, 2002.

Schmidt, Cynthia. *Colorado: Grassroots.* Phoenix: Cloud Publishing, 2000.

Simmons, Virginia McConnell. *The Ute Indians of Utah, Colorado and New Mexico.* Boulder: University Press of Colorado, 2000.

Index